GENERAL VENTILATION IN THE WORKPLACE

GUIDANCE FOR EMPLOYERS

HSG202

HSE
BOOKS

©Crown copyright 2000
Applications for reproduction should be made in
writing to:
Copyright Unit, Her Majesty's Stationery Office,
St. Clements House, 2-16 Colegate,
Norwich NR3 1BQ
First published 2000

ISBN 0 7176 1793 9

This guidance is issued by the Health and
Safety Executive. Following the guidance is
not compulsory and you are free to take other
action. But if you do follow the guidance you
will normally be doing enough to comply with
the law. Health and safety inspectors seek to
secure compliance with the law and may refer
to this guidance as illustrating good practice.

CONTENTS

INTRODUCTION

1   Everyone working in offices, shops, factories, hospitals, laboratories etc requires a minimum standard of fresh air to produce a healthy working environment. One way that this can be provided is by effective general ventilation. This guidance is aimed at employers to help them understand the benefits and limitations of effective general ventilation in the workplace.

2   This guide defines general ventilation and gives information on fresh air requirements. It also looks at the principles and use of general ventilation as a means of controlling exposure to substances hazardous to health as required under the Control of Substances Hazardous to Health Regulations (COSHH) 1999[1] and the associated Approved Codes of Practice.[2] It gives the current ventilation standards and advises you, the employer, on how to achieve effective general ventilation in your workplace. It outlines the methods used to assess the effectiveness of your ventilation system and sets out the legislation on what you are required to do to ensure effective ventilation. The guide also tells you where to get further information and help.

3   This guide does not deal with ventilation of:

▲ processes requiring local exhaust ventilation (LEV);

▲ some specialised premises, for example livestock buildings, confined spaces, mines or flammable stores; or

▲ domestic premises.

4   This guide does not deal with systems for controlling smoke and combustion products from accidental fires or the consequences of condensation and mould growth.

WHAT IS GENERAL VENTILATION?

5   General ventilation or 'dilution' ventilation is a term used to define the flow of air into and out of a working area, for example an office space, so that any contaminants are diluted by adding some fresh air. This can be provided by:

▲ N*atural ventilation* which relies on wind pressure and temperature differences to move fresh air through a building and is usually not fully controllable; and

▲ '*Forced' or mechanical* ventilation which uses mechanical supply and/or extraction to provide fresh air and is controllable (see Figure 1).

WHY IS FRESH AIR REQUIRED IN THE WORKPLACE?

6   You need to provide fresh air to:

▲ provide oxygen for breathing in and to remove carbon dioxide from breathing out;

▲ remove excess heat or, if conditioned, provide heat eg in winter and keep a comfortable temperature;

▲ dilute and remove body and other types of odours (eg food); and

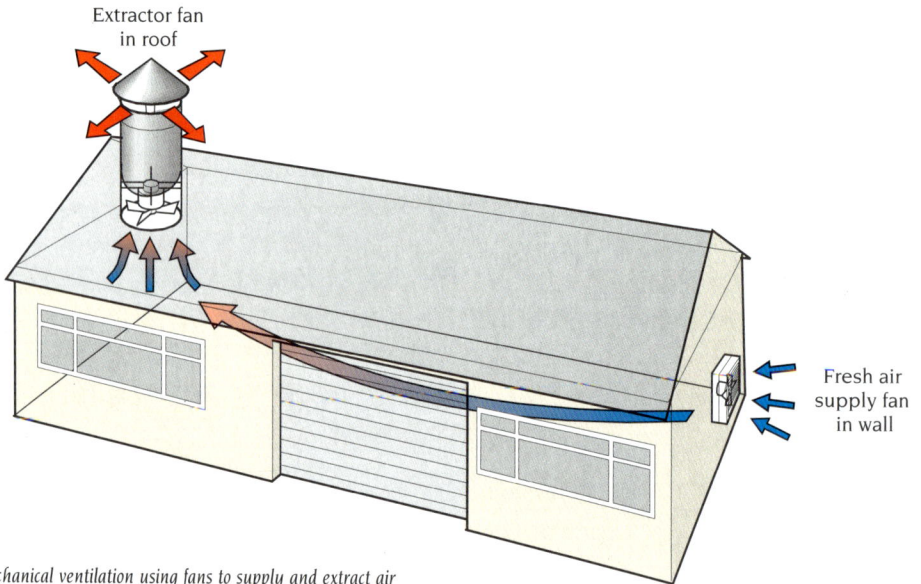

Figure 1: Mechanical ventilation using fans to supply and extract air

▲ dilute any contaminants caused by workplace activities (ie the use of 'dilution' ventilation following a risk assessment).

7 Fresh air is 'clean' air which has come from a source outside the workplace. The main constituents of dry air by volume are:

▲ nitrogen	78.08%
▲ oxygen	20.94%
▲ inert gases	0.95%
▲ carbon dioxide	0.03%
	(300 parts per million)

8 The 'fresh air' which is brought into your workplace should be free of contaminants such as engine exhaust emissions, or discharges from oil or gas fired flues or extract outlets. If you expect the inlet air to be heavily contaminated with particulates (eg heavy traffic, smoke etc) then it should be filtered. Air to be recirculated should be adequately filtered to remove particulates, and should have fresh air added to it before being reintroduced into the workplace.

9 When providing fresh air for your employees, make sure there are no uncomfortable draughts from the movement of air.

Health effects of insufficient fresh air

10 Insufficient fresh air may lead to tiredness, lethargy, headaches, dry or itchy skin and eye irritation in your employees. These symptoms may also be produced whilst working in poorly designed buildings and offices and where there are unsatisfactory working conditions, for example the inability of workers to control certain aspects of their work. The symptoms are generally worse in buildings where there is not enough fresh air. These are common symptoms of what is generally known as 'sick building syndrome' (SBS).

11 The HSE publication *How to deal with sick building syndrome*[3] gives information on the causes of SBS and guidance on how to prevent it.

PRINCIPLES OF NATURAL VENTILATION

12 A basic knowledge of the principles of natural ventilation can help you understand how to use general ventilation as a way of controlling exposure to contaminants produced in the workplace.

13 Natural ventilation is produced by the effects of temperature and changes in air pressure ie wind. Temperature and air pressure differences in a building create an upward movement of air or 'stack' effect. Occasionally, there can be downward air movement if the air is cold.

14 Wind forces are affected by wind speed, wind direction and the shape of the building. Cross-ventilation occurs when wind blows air through a room or building which has openings, for example windows on opposite sides (see Figure 2). Single-sided ventilation occurs when there are one or more openings (such as a window and a door) on one side only.

15 Stack ventilation may be effective enough to carry vapours generated by small-scale hot industrial processes upwards. They can then be removed through the roof via roof

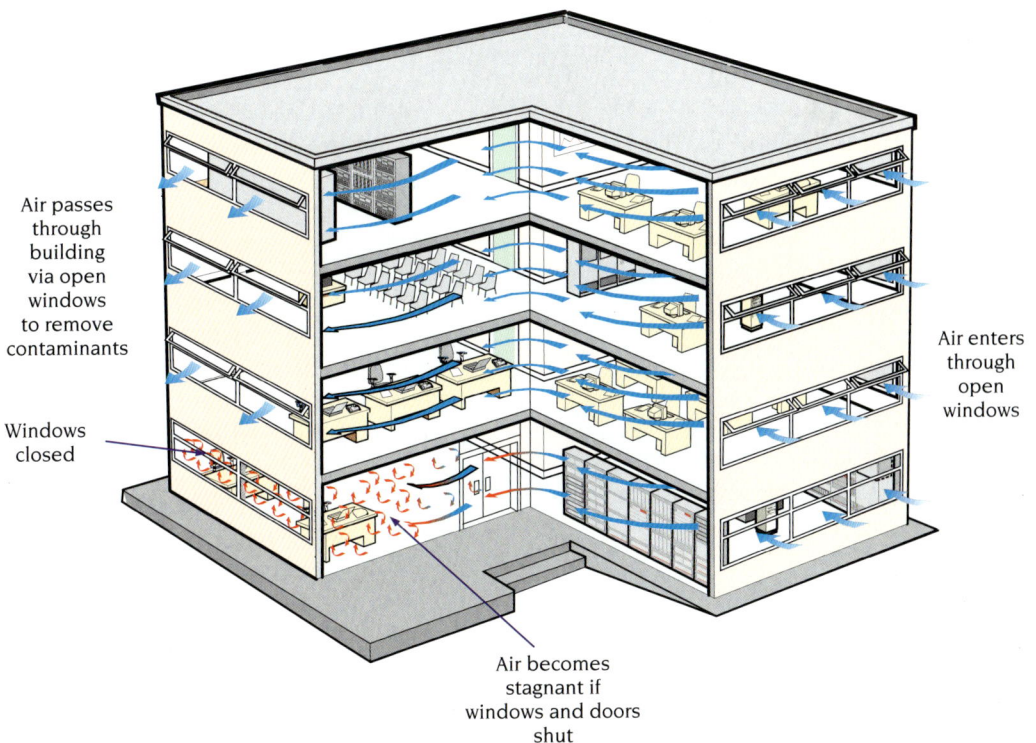

Air passes through building via open windows to remove contaminants

Windows closed

Air enters through open windows

Air becomes stagnant if windows and doors shut

Figure 2: Cross-ventilation to remove contaminants in an office building

Vapour laden air rises to roof where it accumulates or escapes through roof vent

If ventilation is not sufficient, the vapour will collect in the roof space or drift back down

Vapour which does not escape may hang in stratified layer

Cool air enters at low level through open windows

Cool air enters at low level through open windows

Hot process producing fumes

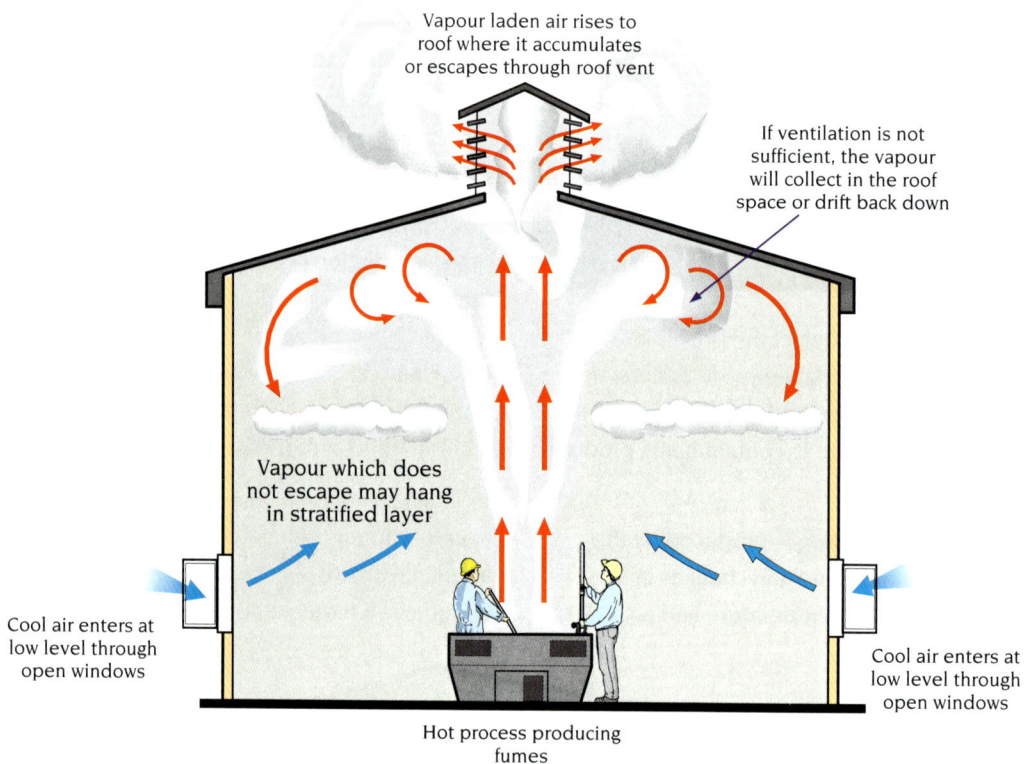

Figure 3: Stack ventilation to remove vapours through roof ventilators

ventilators or extraction fans. If cooler air comes in at a low level, it will displace the warm rising contaminated air, ie displacement ventilation (see paragraph 20)(see Figure 3).

WHEN TO USE GENERAL VENTILATION

16 To ensure a well ventilated workplace you should provide general ventilation that removes stale, contaminated, or hot and humid air so that your employees do not suffer any ill-health effects. There is guidance on how you can ensure thermal comfort at your workplace in the

HSE publication *Thermal comfort in the workplace.*[4]

17 You may consider using effective natural and/or mechanical general ventilation to provide the fresh air supply.

18 As an employer, if you carry out industrial or non-industrial work processes (eg hairdressing, catering) you will be required to undertake a risk assessment under the COSHH Regulations. This means assessing the risks to health of your employees who may be potentially exposed to substances hazardous to health. You may then need to prevent or adequately control such exposure.

4

19 If the contaminant is of such a low toxicity and produced in such low concentrations that it would be impractical and costly to use local exhaust ventilation, you may decide to use general ventilation as part of your control strategy (see HSE publication COSHH *Essentials*).[5] However, if there are a small number of well-spaced contaminant sources, using LEV may be more cost effective than general ventilation (see Figure 4). There may be instances where intermittent exposure to a substance exceeds the assigned Occupational Exposure Limit (OEL), for example during welding and paint spraying. In this case, you should consider using LEV to control exposure.

20 When you use general ventilation to control exposure to contaminants generated from industrial processes, it is essential that:

▲ the rate of contaminant produced is low enough for it to be effectively diluted by the airflow rate;

▲ the contaminant has a low toxicity (see the Chemicals (Hazard Information and Packaging for Supply) (Amendment) Regulations 1999[6]);

▲ the contaminant is produced at a uniform rate;

▲ the workers are positioned at 90° to the air flow (the contaminant air must not be drawn or blown towards the faces of the operatives);

▲ the contaminant is generated in low concentrations and can be controlled to the assigned OEL (see HSE publication EH40/2000[7]); and

▲ the air flow does not affect the performance of other extraction systems eg fume cupboards, LEV.

Use of recirculated air

21 You may want to use recirculated air to conserve energy costs. The extracted air

Dilution ventilation removes any airborne contaminants when lids are removed

Local exhaust ventilation is used to control hazardous substances

Figure 4: A factory using a combination of local exhaust ventilation and dilution ventilation to control airborne contaminants

returned to the workroom can be provided by mechanical ventilation such as an air-conditioning system. Conditioning includes heating or cooling the air, filtering it and, in some cases, adjusting the humidity to provide the most comfortable working conditions (see Figure 5).

22 This treatment is unlikely to remove all contaminants. In some cases they may reach such high concentrations that they cause health problems. This means that you should provide an adequate supply of air into the system at a sufficient rate to replace lost air. This way you can dilute the contaminants using the correct fresh air supply rate.

Emergencies

23 You must use a risk assessment to decide how to manage an emergency. This could be a spillage or release of a substance hazardous to health, which may be a mist, vapour, gas, fume or dust, into the atmosphere. Depending on the level of risk you may then use general ventilation to dilute the air, for instance opening a window to provide rapid ventilation of the environment.

24 However, when your employees enter an emergency area for cleaning up they should use other control measures, for example wearing suitable respiratory protective equipment to protect them from potential exposure to hazardous substances.

25 If necessary, ventilation systems which recirculate air must be switched off to reduce the risk of fire and explosion during the emergency.

STANDARDS OF GENERAL VENTILATION

26 The Workplace (Health, Safety and Welfare) Regulations 1992 (WHSW),[8] regulation 6 requires that you, the employer, do what is needed to make sure that every enclosed workplace is ventilated by a sufficient quantity of fresh or purified air.

27 The Guidance[9] for regulation 6 states that the fresh air supply rate to your workplace should not normally fall below **5 to 8 litres per second, per occupant.** You need to consider several factors when deciding the appropriate rate for your workplace.

These include:

▲ the amount of floor space available per occupant;

▲ the work activity;

▲ the smoking habits of the occupants; and

▲ whether there are other sources of airborne contamination arising from process machinery, heaters, furniture, furnishings etc.

Factories, hospitals, laboratories etc

28 If you use general ventilation to control exposure to a substance hazardous to health, it is important that you choose the right air supply rate. This should reduce the concentrations of the contaminants to well below the appropriate OELs or to a safe level where OELs are not specified so as to protect your employees from ill health.

29 In this case, it is advisable to consult an occupational hygienist and/or a ventilation

Full recirculation
(with conditioning)

Motorised dampers to control
fresh air intake and exhaust

The use of fresh air
and recirculated air

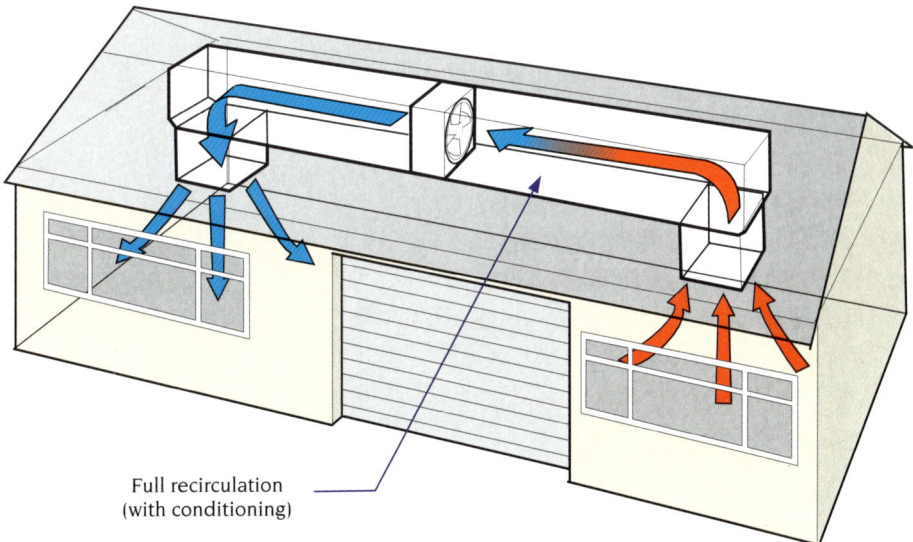

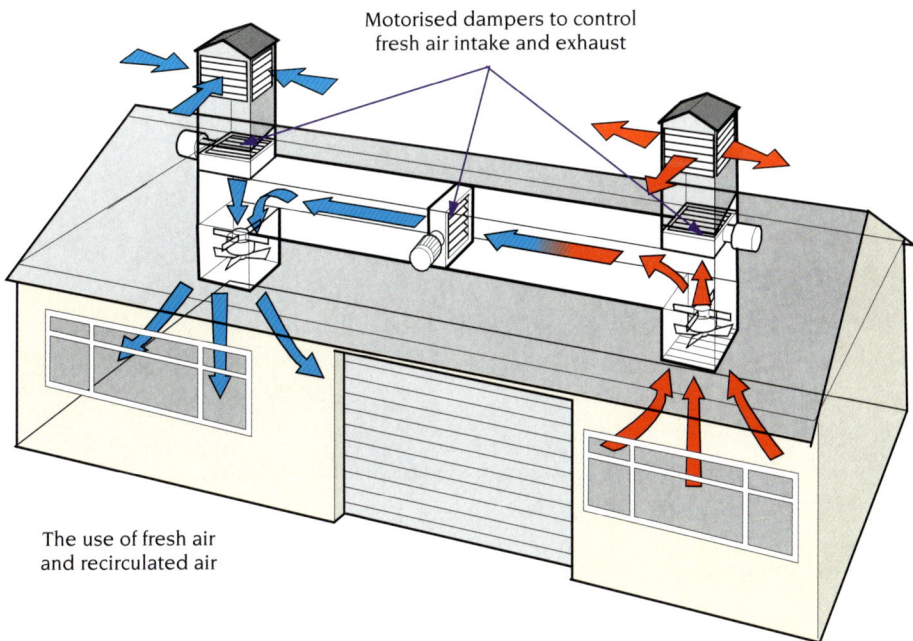

Figure 5: Examples of recirculation systems

engineer or other competent person to decide on the correct ventilation rate and design.

Offices, shops, theatres etc

30 Employees in offices, shops and in the entertainment industry are exposed to contaminants arising from many sources including carpets, furniture, cleaning products, heaters, photocopiers, the building itself, the ventilation ducting and from the outside environment.

31 General ventilation is needed to remove odours, in particular body odours from people, rather than to reduce adverse health effects.

32 The recommended fresh air supply rates per person are given in the CIBSE *Guide* A: *Environmental Design*[10] produced by the Chartered Institution of Building Services Engineers (CIBSE). These are based on diluting personal odour and cigarette smoke even though many companies now operate a 'no smoking' policy or allocate separate smoking areas.

33 A recommended fresh air supply rate of **8 litres per second per person** should provide a clean and hygienic workplace in open plan offices, shops and even factories. Higher fresh air supply rates of **up to 36 litres per second per person** are recommended for heavily contaminated buildings ie 70% of people smoking (see CIBSE Guide A[10]).

Standards for gas, coal or oil fired equipment

34 If you use gas, coal or oil fired equipment, the fresh air requirements will depend on what kind of flue arrangement you use. Room ventilation rates can vary considerably for open flue (drawing air from the room and discharging products outside) and unflued appliances (drawing air from and discharging products into the room). Further details are given in the relevant British Standards (see Further Information).

35 Your workers are at risk of gas poisoning, in particular from carbon monoxide, if there is not enough fresh air in the room to remove combustion products, especially from unflued combustion equipment. It is essential that all appliances are expertly installed and receive regular maintenance and servicing by a competent person.

Air movement

36 Air movement caused by general ventilation can affect comfortable working conditions. Your workers will be happier if they can alter their environment, for example by opening or shutting a window when required. **At normal temperatures an air flow velocity of between 0.1 to 0.15 metres per second and up to 0.25 metres per second during the summer** is recommended by CIBSE.[10] Keep draughts to a minimum.

HOW TO ACHIEVE EFFECTIVE VENTILATION IN YOUR WORKPLACE

37 If your workplace is appropriately designed, for example by providing space for flexibility, and if the building is situated where there is enough shade to minimise summer heat, then you should be able to obtain adequate natural ventilation.

38 In most buildings make up air (air to replace that lost from the building) will be supplied indirectly through gaps around doors and window frames or directly through vents, windows, grilles and open doors.

39 But there are things you can do to make sure you have effective ventilation in your workplace:

▲ install trickle ventilators in window frames as well as having windows that open to provide controllable draught free ventilation (it is important that in winter any windows are well sealed and secure when closed) (see Figure 6);

▲ keep doors and windows open to provide a good supply of make up air (in winter when the doors and windows are shut, you can supply make up air through air vents and extract any contaminated air using a suitable system eg via roof vents);

▲ position fans to extract contaminated air through an extraction point downwind or to supply fresh air on a wall and/or in the roof, in particular if your workplace has a large internal space (as in many industrial units, garages and warehouses);

▲ use fans on the wall of each side of the building to keep fresh air flowing

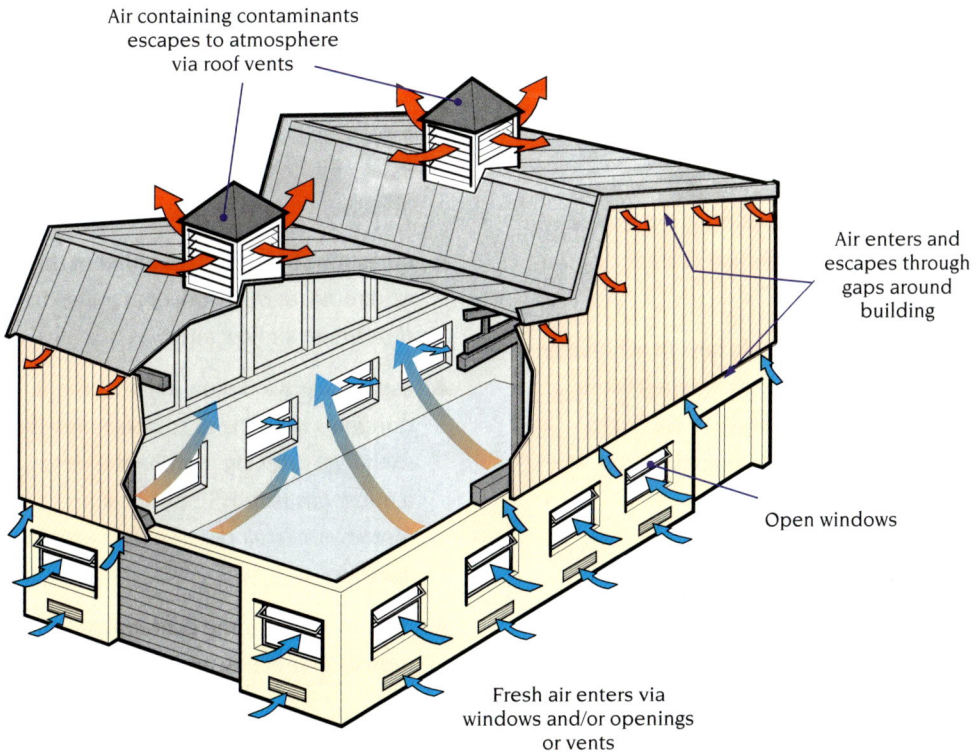

Air containing contaminants escapes to atmosphere via roof vents

Air enters and escapes through gaps around building

Open windows

Fresh air enters via windows and/or openings or vents

Figure 6: Natural ventilation moving fresh air through a building

throughout the building ie one extracting the contaminated air while the other supplies fresh air (make sure your employees work between the air supply and contaminant source). For example, in mortuaries fresh air should be provided by an inlet located in the ceiling and extracted at a low level outlet to reduce the risk of microbes being inhaled;

▲ use a combination of extraction fans in the wall and/or roof, with open windows and doors to supply make up air;

▲ discharge any exhausted air above the roof and make sure that there is no opening for supply air near the exhaust discharge making allowance for wind effects; and

▲ locate any exhaust fans as near the source of the contamination as possible.

40 Situate any extract and supply fan to make sure that there is enough air movement to remove stale and contaminated air from all parts of the room or building. Otherwise you may create poorly ventilated areas or 'dead zones'.

41 You can use portable fans to achieve an adequate air flow at specific sites within a building to keep employees cool or to remove contaminants generated from a particular process.

42 To keep internal conditions constant or to keep a process clean from airborne contaminants you can use a more complex mechanical system where the air is recirculated after being filtered.

ASSESSING THE EFFECTIVENESS OF YOUR VENTILATION SYSTEM

43 When required, your initial assessment (see paragraph 18) should start with information on your workplace layout, the number of your employees and their views on the ventilation provided, the likely source of pollution, evidence of draughts, thermal conditions and the types of ventilation system you are using. Once you have collected this data you can then assess whether the ventilation systems you use provide sufficient fresh air.

44 Various techniques can be used to assess the effectiveness of building ventilation systems ranging from the simple smoke test to the more complex measurement of tracer gas.

Examples include:

▲ using smoke tubes to visualise the pattern of air movement in a workplace;

▲ measuring air velocities either in the workroom, in ductwork or at grilles to determine air flow rates;

▲ using tracers to follow air movement through a building or to determine the air exchange rates by plotting the decay rate of a tracer gas (see HSE publication *Measurement of air change rates in factories and offices*[11]);

▲ monitoring airborne contaminants from an industrial process; and

▲ measuring carbon dioxide concentration within the workplace; levels over 1,000 ppm may indicate inadequate ventilation (see CIBSE *Guidance Note Healthy Workplaces*[12]).

45 **Ventilation monitoring using tracers or airborne contaminants is a specialised technique and should be carried out by people with the right expertise and equipment, for example occupational hygienists.**

Maintenance of mechanical ventilation systems

46 The ACOP to regulation 6 of the WHSW Regulations 1992[9] requires that any mechanical ventilation systems, including air conditioning systems, which you use to provide fresh air should be regularly and properly cleaned, tested and maintained to make sure that they are kept clean and free from anything which may contaminate the air and cause health problems.

47 As a general rule, if you run your finger along the opening of a duct and it collects dust then it probably needs cleaning. Organisations such as the Heating and Ventilating Contractors Association (HVCA) and the Chartered Institution of Building Services Engineers (CIBSE) provide information on testing for likely contaminants in ductwork and on cleaning.

48 If you provide general ventilation by mechanical systems to reduce concentrations of contaminants in the workplace environment which would otherwise cause ill health, then regulation 6 (2) of the WHSW Regulations 1992[8] states that you will need to include an effective visible or audible alarm to warn of a failure in the system.

WHAT THE LAW REQUIRES YOU TO DO

49 **The Health and Safety at Work etc Act 1974,**[13] **Section 2 (2) (e)** requires that you, as an employer, provide and maintain a working environment that is, so far as is reasonably practicable, safe and without risk to health.

50 **The Control of Substances Hazardous to Health Regulations 1999**[1] **(COSHH) regulations 6,7 and 8** require that you undertake a risk assessment and prevent or control the exposure of your employees to substances hazardous to health by using suitable control measures which includes general ventilation. Maintenance, examination and testing of the control measures (for example general ventilation) to meet the requirements of **regulation 7** are covered by **regulation 9**.

51 **The Workplace (Health, Safety and Welfare) Regulations 1992,**[8] **regulation 5** requires that mechanical ventilation systems used for providing general ventilation are maintained (including cleaned as appropriate) in an efficient state, in efficient working order and in good repair. **Regulation 6** requires that you ensure effective ventilation for any enclosed workplace by providing a sufficient quantity of fresh or purified air. The associated Approved Code of Practice and Guidance[9] gives you practical guidance. Note that it does not specify how you can achieve effective ventilation but refers you to more detailed guidance elsewhere.

52 Also, **regulations 21 and 25** require that you, the employer, ensure that toilets are well ventilated so that offensive odours do not linger and that rest rooms and rest areas include suitable arrangements to protect non-smokers from discomfort caused by smoking.

53 Under the **Safety Representatives and Safety Committees Regulations 1977**[14] and the **Health and Safety (Consultation with Employees) Regulations 1996,**[15] information on the control measures used including general ventilation should be made available to the employees.

REFERENCES

1 The Control of Substances Hazardous to Health Regulations 1999 SI 1999/437 Stationery Office 1999 ISBN 0 11 082087 8

2 General COSHH ACOP (Control of substances hazardous to health) and Carcinogens ACOP (Control of carcinogenic substances) and Biological agents ACOP (Control of biological agents).
Control of Substances Hazardous to Health Regulations 1999. Approved Codes of Practice L5 HSE Books 1999 ISBN 0 7176 1670 3

3 How to deal with SBS sick building syndrome: Guidance for employers, building owners and building managers HSG132 HSE Books 1995 ISBN 0 7176 0861 1

4 Thermal comfort in the workplace HSG194 HSE Books 1999 ISBN 0 7176 2468 4

5 COSHH Essentials: Easy steps to control chemicals HSG193 HSE Books 1999 ISBN 0 7176 2421 8

6 Chemicals Hazard Information & Packaging for Supply (Amendment) Regulations 1997 SI 1997/1460 Stationery Office 1997 ISBN 0 11 063750 X

7 Occupational Exposure Limits Guidance Note EH40/2000 HSE Books 2000 ISBN 0 7176 1315 1

8 The Workplace (Health, Safety and Welfare) Regulations 1992 SI 1992/3004 HMSO 1992 ISBN 0 11 025804 5

9 Workplace health, safety and welfare. Workplace (Health, Safety and Welfare) Regulations 1992: Approved Code of Practice and guidance L24 HSE Books 1992 ISBN 0 7176 0413 6

10 CIBSE Guide: Volume A: Environmental design CIBSE 1999 ISBN 0 900953 95 0

11 Measurement of air change rates in factories and offices MDHS 73 HMSO 1992 ISBN 0 11 885 693 6

12 Healthy Workplaces: Guidance to complying with the 1992 health and safety regulations CIBSE Guidance Note GN2: 1993 ISBN 0 900953 58 6

13 The Health and Safety at Work etc Act 1974 CH37 HMSO ISBN 0 10 543774 3

14 The Safety Representatives and Safety Committees Regulations 1977 SI 1977/500 HMSO 1997 ISBN 0 11 070500 9

15 The Health and Safety (Consultation with Employees) Regulations 1996 SI 1996/1513 HMSO 1996 ISBN 0 11 054839 6

FURTHER INFORMATION

HSE publications

Approved Supply List (5th edition). Information approved for the classification and labelling of substances and preparations dangerous for supply. Chemicals (Hazard Information and Packaging for Supply)(Amendment) Regulations 1994 (as amended). Approved List. HSE Books 1999 ISBN 0 7176 1725 4

Safety in the installation and use of gas systems and appliances. Gas Safety (Installation and Use) Regulations 1994. Approved Code of Practice and guidance L56 HSE Books 1994 ISBN 0 7176 1635 5

Maintenance, examination and testing of local exhaust ventilation 2nd edition HSG54 HSE Books 1998 ISBN 0 7176 1485 9

Ventilation of kitchens in catering establishments HSE Information Sheet: Catering Sheet No 10 HSE Books 1997

The control of legionellosis including legionnaires disease 2nd edition HSG70 HSE Books 1993 ISBN 0 7176 0451 9

An introduction to local exhaust ventilation HSG37 HMSO 1993 ISBN 0 11 882134 2

Passive smoking at work: Workplace air pollution INDG63REV HMSO 1992

British Standards Institution publications

Code of practice for mechanical ventilation and air conditioning in buildings BS 5720:1979 British Standards Institution 1979 ISBN 05801 071 83

Code of practice for ventilation principles and designing for natural ventilation BS 5925:1991 British Standards Institution 1991 ISBN 05801 928 57

Installation of flues and ventilation for gas appliances of rated input not exceeding 60 kW (1st, 2nd and 3rd family gases). Part 1. Specification for installation of flues BS 5440: Part 1: 1990 British Standards Institution 1990 ISBN 05801 81421

Installation of flues and ventilation for gas appliances of rated input not exceeding 60 kW (1st, 2nd and 3rd family gases). Part 2. Specification for installation of ventilation for gas appliances BS 5440: Part 2: 1989 British Standards Institution 1989 ISBN 05801 80050

Other publications

CIBSE Guide: Volume B: Installation and equipment data 5th edition CIBSE 1986 ISBN 0 900953 30 6

CIBSE Guide: Volume C: Reference data 5th edition CIBSE 1986 ISBN 0 90053 31 4

CIBSE Hygiene maintenance of office ventilation ductwork TM26:1999 CIBSE 2000 (to be published later this year)

The Building Regulations 1991. F1 Means of ventilation. F2 Condensation in roofs HMSO 1994 ISBN 0 11 752932 X

CIBSE Minimising pollution at air intakes - TM21: 1999 CISBE 1999 ISBN 0900 953 91 8

CIBSE Natural ventilation in non-domestic buildings - Applications Manual AM 10: 1997 CIBSE 1997 ISBN 0 000953 77 2

American Society of Heating, Refrigerating and Air-conditioning Engineers Inc *Ventilation for acceptable indoor air quality* ASHRAE Standard 62-1989 ASHRAE 1989
ISSN 1041 2336

TR/17 *Guide to good practice - Cleanliness of ventilation systems* Heating and Ventilating Contractors' Association 1998
ISBN 0 9037 83 26 6

The American Conference of Governmental Industrial Hygienists *Industrial ventilation. A manual of recommended practice.* 23rd Edition (Metric Version) 1998 ISBN 1 882417 26 7

While every effort has been made to ensure the accuracy of the references listed in this publication, their future availability cannot be guaranteed.

Useful organisations

The following organisations produce general information, guides, and standards on general ventilation:

The Heating and Ventilating Contractors Association (HVCA), tel: 020 7229 2488 publishes guidance on testing and maintenance.

The British Occupational Hygiene Society (BOHS), tel: 01332 298101 has produced a general guide on controlling hazardous substances in the workplace, *Technical Guide No 7: Controlling airborne contaminants in the workplace.*

The British Institute of Occupational Hygienists (BIOH) tel: 01332 298087 provide information on occupational hygiene, including general ventilation.

British Standards are available from BSI Customer Services, 389 Chiswick High Road, London W4 4AL. Tel: 020 8996 9001. Fax: 020 8996 7001.

The Chartered Institution of Building Services Engineers (CIBSE), tel: 020 8675 5211 publishes various technical guides on building design and general ventilation for example the applications manual *Natural ventilation in non-domestic buildings* (see above) which provides guidance on how to ensure natural ventilation, standards etc.

The Building Services Research and Information Association (BSRIA), tel: 01344 426511 publishes technical documents on general ventilation and provides information.

The Building Research Establishment (BRE), tel: 01923 894040 publishes technical guidance on general ventilation.

The American Society of Heating, Refrigerating and Air-conditioning Engineers Inc (ASHRAE) can be contacted on tel: 001 404 636 8400.

Printed and published by the Health and Safety Executive   C80   6/00